#  CONTENTS

# ITALY: PAST AND PRESENT

## A Roman history

The Italian city of Rome was once the biggest and most important city in Europe. This was during the 1st and 2nd centuries AD, when the **Roman Empire** stretched from Britain in the west to Syria in the east. By the 5th century, the empire had been broken up and Rome itself was attacked by invaders from central Europe. In Italy today there are ruins of Roman buildings, a network of Roman roads and parts of the Latin language left to remind us of the Roman Empire.

*The remains of the Colosseum in Rome.*
- *This was built in AD72 to hold games, contests and races.*
- *Up to 50,000 people could watch the events.*

## City states

Throughout the Middle Ages and up until the middle of the 19th century, Italy was made up of many small **states** with a city at the centre of each. Cities such as Florence, Venice and Genoa were separate **city states**. These cities became rich, mostly because of trade. Merchants from Florence, for example, made their fortunes by **exporting** large quantities of fine woollen cloth. During the 9th and 10th centuries, all these states and most of the rest of Europe were part of the Holy Roman Empire. The Pope in Rome was its religious leader.

*The ancient city of Siena in Tuscany.*
- *People wear medieval costumes and carry banners at the start of the Palio bareback horse-race.*
- *The race has been run since the 14th century.*

# Italy

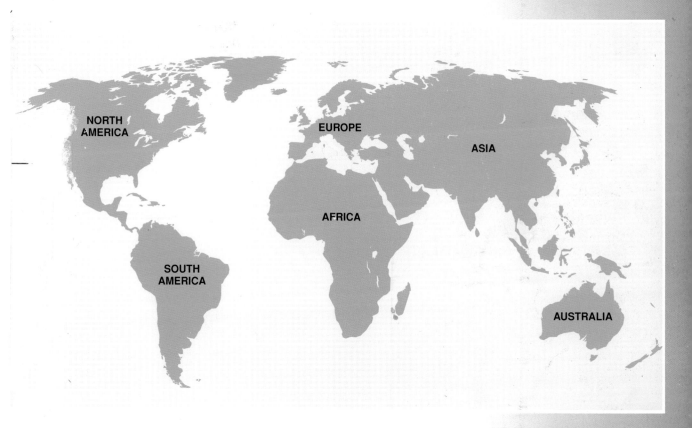

NORTH AMERICA

EUROPE

ASIA

AFRICA

SOUTH AMERICA

AUSTRALIA

## Fred Martin

Heinemann
LIBRARY

First published in Great Britain by Heinemann Library
Halley Court, Jordan Hill, Oxford OX2 8EJ
a division of Reed Educational and Professional Publishing Ltd

OXFORD FLORENCE PRAGUE MADRID ATHENS
MELBOURNE AUCKLAND KUALA LUMPUR SINGAPORE TOKYO
IBADAN NAIROBI KAMPALA JOHANNESBURG GABORONE
PORTSMOUTH NH CHICAGO MEXICO CITY SAO PAULO

Designed by AMR
Illustrations by Art Construction
Printed in Hong Kong by Wing King Tong Company Limited.

02 01 00 99
10 9 8 7 6 5 4 3 2

ISBN 0 431 01349 7

This title is also available in a hardback library edition (ISBN 0 431 01348 9).

**British Library Cataloguing in Publication Data**

Martin, Fred, 1948-
Next Stop Italy
1. Italy – Geography – Juvenile literature
I.Title  II.Italy
914.5

**Acknowledgements**
The Publishers would like to thank the following for permission to reproduce photographs:
J Allan Cash Ltd pp.9, 10, 22; Trevor Clifford pp.12, 13, 15, 16, 17, 18, 21, 24, 27; Colorific!
B. & C. Alexander p.7, J. Blair p.11; Katz Pictures G. Berengo p.23, G. B. Gardin p.25, C. Paone
p.28; Trip B. Gadsby pp.7, 26, J. Moscrop p.8, C. Rennie pp.4, 19, H. Rogers p.4, H. Rooney p.29,
E. Smith pp.14, 20.

Cover photograph reproduced with permission of Tristan Boyer.

Our thanks to Anna Samuels for her comments in the preparation of this book.

Every effort has been made to contact holders of any material reproduced in this book. Any
omissions will be rectified in subsequent printings if notice is given to the Publisher.

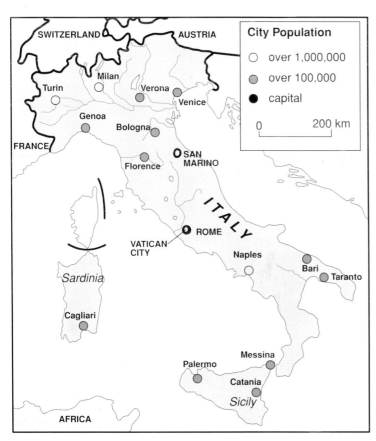

## Italy unites

Italy remained divided into a patchwork of different countries, some parts at times ruled by Spain, France and Austria, until 1861. In 1861, the different states joined together to become a united Italy. They were united by a soldier named Giuseppe [juice-EPeh] Garibaldi.

Between 1922 and 1943, Italy was ruled by a **dictator** named Benito Mussolini even though there was a king. Italy fought in World War II on the same side as Germany. Mussolini was killed as the war was being lost. In 1946, the people of Italy voted to make Italy a **republic** and King Victor Emmanuel III gave up the throne.

Today, most of the 58 million people who live in Italy have a reasonable **standard of living**. However, a serious problem is that there is more wealth in the north than in the south. Although investment is being made and industries developed in the south, many people are still unemployed and living in poverty there.

**The Vatican City and San Marino never became part of the new Italy when it formed in 1861. They are still independent, self-governing countries inside Italy's borders.**

# THE NATURAL LANDSCAPE

## Peninsula and islands

Italy is almost completely surrounded by the sea. It is a long, narrow **peninsula** stretching 1000 kilometres out into the Mediterranean Sea. At its widest point the distance across the peninsula is about 240 kilometres. The two islands of Sicily and Sardinia and some smaller islands, such as Capri, are also part of Italy.

## Mountains, volcanoes and earthquakes

About three-quarters of Italy is either mountainous or hilly. The Alps in the north rise to heights of over 4500 metres. The highest peak in the Italian Alps is *Monte Rosa* at 4634 metres.

*Monte Bianco* is shared with France where it is called *Mont Blanc*. (The words *bianco* and *blanc* both mean white.) The Dolomites is a mountain range in the eastern part of the Alps. These mountains rise to about 3300 metres and are very steep and rocky.

The Apennines mountain chain runs almost the whole length of Italy's peninsula. At an average of about 2000 metres, its mountains are not as high or as steep as the Alps. In some places, their slopes drop straight down into the sea.

Mount Vesuvius is the only **active volcano** on the mainland of Europe. It last erupted in 1944. Mount Etna, on the Italian island of Sicily, is Europe's highest active volcano at 3340 metres. **Lava** from Mount Etna sometimes flows quickly down the slopes and destroys people's homes and farms.

There are also **earthquakes** in Italy. Unlike volcanoes, earthquakes can happen anywhere in the country.

Mt Rosa 4634

Mt Bianco

ALPS

R. Po

ITALY

R. Tiber

APENNINES

ADRIATIC SEA

Mt Vesuvius ▲

Sardinia

TYRRHENIAN SEA

MEDITERRANEAN SEA

Mt Etna 3340

Sicily

**Height in metres**

over 1000
500–1000
200–500
0–200

0        200 km

*The Monte Bianco in the Valle d'Aosta region of Italy.*
- *The sharp Alpine peaks and deep valleys have been shaped by ice and valley glaciers.*
- *Many of the people in Valle d'Aosta speak French as well as Italian.*

*An abandoned village in Calabria in the south of Italy.*
- *Earthquakes have made many hilltop villages too dangerous to live in.*

## Lowlands and rivers

The largest area of lowland is in the north. The River Po and its **tributaries** flow from the Alps across this wide and flat plain. Further south, smaller and shorter rivers, such as the Tiber, flow east into the Adriatic Sea and west into the Tyrrhenian Sea. Some of the smaller rivers stop flowing during the long hot summer months. There is not enough rain or water in the ground to keep them flowing.

**Volcanoes are named after an island near Sicily called Vulcano. This was said to be where the Roman god Vulcan lived. Vulcan was the blacksmith who used fire to make swords for other gods.**

# CLIMATE, VEGETATION AND WILDLIFE

### Climate – north to south

Italy is one of the most southerly countries in Europe. This is the main reason why much of Italy has a climate that is warmer and drier than countries further north. This type of climate is called a **Mediterranean climate**.

Yet because the north and south of Italy are so far apart, they have different climates. In the north, you can expect rain all year round. In winter, the **average temperature** is not much above **freezing point**. The coldest and wettest places are in the Alps. In summer, it becomes very hot with an average temperature of about 25°C. There are also violent thunderstorms in late summer. In 1994 at least 60 people died when the area suffered its worst storms for 80 years.

Summer near Venice in north-east Italy.
- *This hot and dry weather makes the Adriatic coast one of Italy's main tourist areas.*

8

*Mount Etna on the island of Sicily.*
- *Short grasses, low bushes and scattered trees grow in this hot and dry part of Italy.*

The south of Italy is sometimes called the *mezzogiorno* [METso-JORno], which means midday, because a major feature of the area is the heat of the midday sun. If you visit Palermo in Sicily you can expect the weather to be warm even in winter, at about 10°C. It is much hotter in summer at about 35°C. There is rain in the winter but there is a **drought** with almost no rain in the summer.

## A changing landscape

People have been farming and building in Italy for thousands of years so there is not much natural vegetation left. Oak, beech and pine trees once covered most of the land, but there is little woodland now. Even the marshes have been drained and made into farmland. Low bushes and scrub grow where the soil is thin and stony. This type of area is called *maquis* or *garrigue*.

## Wild animals

There are not many large wild animals left in Italy. There are some brown bears in the Alps and in the forests of Calabria in the south. Wolves also live in these remote areas and wild boar live on the island of Sardinia. Deer, the rare chamois goat, and wild sheep called mouflon can still be seen. Most of these rare animals are now protected.

**Large areas of the Apennines are bleak places. Dry and barren, they are covered with scrub instead of trees. Goats have overgrazed the hills. Each summer there are serious forest fires when the parched scrub catches fire.**

# TOWNS AND CITIES

### Historic Rome

Many of the towns and cities in Italy were first built up by the ancient Romans. There are many reminders of the city's ancient history, such as the Colosseum where 50,000 people could watch the gladiators and other entertainments. Other famous old parts of the city were built in the 17th century, such as the many beautiful *piazzas* (squares). Now Rome is a modern **capital city** where almost three million people live. The city is becoming choked with traffic as even more people come to live here.

The Vatican City in Rome is a small independent country of less than half a square kilometre. This is where the Pope lives and where visitors come both to pray and to see the sights.

### Renaissance cities

During the 14th and 15th centuries, towns such as Florence, Pisa and Siena became rich by making and selling goods. This period of history is called the **Renaissance**. Merchants and noblemen paid painters, sculptors and architects to decorate and build fine houses, palaces and churches.

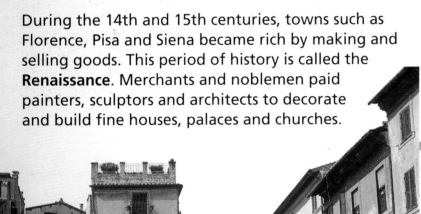

*The Piazza della Rotonda in Rome.*
- *There are many old buildings and piazzas in Italian cities.*
- *The ancient pillar you can see in this picture came from Egypt.*

*Naples is Italy's third largest city with 1,200,000 people.*
- *Naples has been described as being 'a mad jumble of **tenements** and traffic, street **vendors** and crumbling palaces'.*

One of the richest Renaissance cities was Venice. The city was built on small islands and wooden foundations in a lagoon on the edge of the Adriatic Sea. The streets are canals that run between the buildings. Now the weight of the city is making it sink into the mud. Streets and the famous St Mark's Square are sometimes flooded during high tides and storms. Engineers are busy trying to stop their city from sinking into the sea.

## Cities north and south

The main industrial and **commercial** cities such as Milan and Turin are in the north. Historic buildings stand side-by-side with modern office blocks and shops. About seven million people live in Milan and the nearby towns. This is the biggest built-up area in the whole of Italy. People have moved to this area from the poorer regions in the south of Italy.

In the cities in the south, such as Naples and Reggio de Calabria, slum buildings have grown up to house people who have left the country areas in search of work. However, signs of their wealthy Renaissance past, once lost or hidden, are slowly being restored as the cities renovate their beautiful buildings.

**About 30% of all the people in Italy live in the country. In the United Kingdom only 7% of the people live in the country.**

# A FLORENTINE FAMILY

The De Alfieri family outside their apartment.
- Italian families used to have many more children than they do now.

## Living in Florence

Walter and Lucia De Alfieri live in Florence. They have three boys named Vincenzo [vin-CHENzo], Guglielmo [gooly-ELmo] and Federico. The De Alfieri family live in an apartment block in an old building. The old buildings, streets and *piazzas* of Florence give it a character that makes it one of the most beautiful cities in Italy.

Walter and Lucia both have full-time jobs. Walter is a doctor in a local hospital. Lucia works as an editor for a publishing company. This gives the family a high standard of living. Walter and Lucia each own a car, so they can drive to their different places of work.

## The children's life

Vincenzo is aged fourteen. He goes to *Superiore* school while Guglielmo, aged eleven, goes to *Media* school. Lucia drives Federico, who is aged three, to a nursery school. He stays there while Lucia and Walter are at work. After school and at the weekend, the older boys sometimes go to a rowing club in Florence. They are able to row on the River Arno that flows through the city.

Catching the bus to go to school.
- Until now, school was compulsory only up to the age of 14, though most children stayed on.

Lucia buys meat and other foods in a local shop.
- The Tuscany region around Florence is one of the best farming areas in Italy.

*Family life is important to the De Alfieris.*
- *Playing games together is a good way to enjoy each other's company.*

## Recreation and meal times

At home, the family sometimes play board games together. The whole family enjoy reading and there are many books in the De Alfieri home.

Lucia buys most of the family's food in small local shops. There is a good choice of meat, vegetables and other foods. Breakfast is a quick meal of crispbreads, jam and coffee. A typical evening meal would be meat, salad, cheese and pasta. Bread is on the table with every meal. The family eat in the evening at about 8.00 pm. It is much cooler in the evening when the sun has gone down.

The family sometimes go away to the countryside nearby, for the weekend or for longer holidays. They own a second home in the Tuscan countryside. Tuscany is a popular area for both local people and tourists to visit because of the beauty and history of its landscape, towns and villages.

*Guglielmo and Vincenzo go rowing on the River Arno.*
- *The bridge behind them is the famous medieval Ponte Vecchio. It is near the centre of Florence.*

# FARMING LANDSCAPES

## Seen from above

Some people first see Italy as they fly south on the way to a Greek island or an Italian holiday resort on the Adriatic coast. After crossing the Alps, the landscape suddenly flattens into a patchwork of fields. This is the plain of Lombardy where the greatest amount of Italy's farm produce is grown. It is where the soil, climate and **relief** are best for farming.

Wheat, maize and rice are grown in the fields, as are artichokes, peppers, potatoes and melons. Dairy farming is also important in this region. And of course, there are vineyards here as in all parts of Italy. In some years, Italy produces more wine than any other country.

*The farming landscape of Tuscany near Florence.*
- *This area is known for growing grapes that are made into Chianti wine.*
- *Many of the villages were built on hilltops so they could be defended.*

## Poor soil

Further south, the landscape looks very different. Sheep and goats graze on steep hillsides where little can grow except low scrub and short grasses. There are deep **gullies** cut into the hillsides. These are caused as soil is washed away by heavy rain falling on dry bare ground. This is called **soil erosion**. Growing anything is difficult. Villages sit on hilltops where it is cooler. Farmers travel out from the villages to their farms every day.

## Crops in the south

Most of the farms in the south of Italy are very small. The farmers' fields are often scattered over several hillsides. A different type of wheat, called durum wheat, is grown here. This is used to make spaghetti and other types of pasta.

Grapes, tomatoes and olives are grown almost everywhere. Italians use olive oil in much of their cooking. Some of the tomatoes are liquidized on the farm to make tomato sauce. There are also small orchards of **citrus fruits,** such as lemons and oranges.

Crops grow well as long as they can be watered. Without water, crops and other vegetation turn yellow and die. The soil becomes dry and dusty. The method used by people to supply their land with water is called **irrigation**.

*Herding sheep in the south of Italy.*
- *Growing crops and rearing animals is difficult because there is so little rain.*

**One of Italy's most successful exports is tinned food, such as tomatoes. Italy grows over five million tonnes of tomatoes a year.**

# ITALY'S VOLCANIC ISLAND

## Living on Sicily

The Cunsolo family live on the island of Sicily, the biggest island in the Mediterranean Sea. The family run a small farm, but they live in the town of Catania. Catania is an ancient city close to Mount Etna, one of Europe's most active volcanoes. The area also has earthquakes from time to time. The locals have got used to living with these kind of natural hazards.

## The family farm

Most of the work on the orange and olive farm is done by Salvatore Cunsolo. He drives out to the farm which he rents from a landowner. Other members of the family have to help during the harvest. The rent is paid after the crop of oranges and olives has been sold.

Salvatore also works as a part-time painter and decorator. This is because it is impossible to earn enough money by farming with so little land, especially when the prices for oranges and olives are so low. Besides, there are several months in the year when there is no work to do on the farm.

*The Cunsolo family on the balcony of their apartment in Catania.*
- *The buildings are crowded together and most streets are narrow.*

*Salvatore likes to sit outside a café drinking coffee and reading the local newspaper called La Sicilia.*

*The family eating lunch.*
- *The meal consists of pasta followed by stuffed green peppers and aubergines with ricotta cheese.*

## The family home

The family live in a block of flats on the edge of Catania. Salvatore's wife, Anna, works as a supply teacher in a local school. They have four children aged seventeen, thirteen, nine and two. Large families like theirs are typical in the south of Italy. Salvatore's nephew Enrico, also lives with the family.

Zaira, aged nine, goes to her primary school between 8.00 am and 1.00 pm. Her favourite pastime is dancing. Her brother Vincenzo, goes to *Media* school. He enjoys playing football with the other boys at school. Luana, the eldest, goes to college. Enrico works as a dance teacher. He teaches both ballet and contemporary dancing.

Anna shops in the street markets, where she can buy almost anything from food to clothes. Anna is kept very busy preparing food for the family. They enjoy locally grown food, fish and pasta. Eating together is an important part of Italian family life.

*Enrico sometimes helps on the farm.*
- *Picking oranges has to be done by hand.*

*Anna visits the local market to buy most of the family's food.*
- *Some farmers drive to the market and sell their produce straight from their cars.*

*Vincenzo and his friends in the local school enjoy playing football during their break.*

17

# WHAT'S IN ITALIAN SHOPS?

## Big and small

The biggest and most expensive shops in Italy are in the big cities such as Turin, Milan, Naples and Rome. They sell fashionable clothes, shoes and accessories by famous designers. Large, bustling department stores are also found in the centre of these major cities.

In Italy there are also small family-run shops like the *frutterie* that sell fruit, the *panetterie* that sell bread and cakes, and the *gelaterie* that sell ice cream. Tobacconists called *tabaccheria*, also sell stamps.

## Italian specialities

Hand-made goods such as ceramics, lace and pottery are often sold in small shops, especially in areas where there are tourists. Different parts of Italy have their own special products, such as glass ornaments which come from workshops in Venice, leather from Naples and gold jewellery from Florence.

*Buying olives from a stall at the local market, in Sicily.*
- *All the vegetables are grown locally.*

**Leather goods and jewellery can now be bought direct from Italy without ever visiting a shop, or even without visiting Italy. Goods can be viewed and ordered from an Internet web site in Florence.**

## Opening hours

Shops are usually open from 9 am until 1 pm. Many close until about 4 pm and then stay open until about 7 pm. This is to avoid the heat in the middle of the day in summer, especially in the south of Italy. Butchers' shops are sometimes closed on Fridays and on some religious days. This is often done in Roman Catholic countries as a sign of **fasting**.

## Market stalls

Fresh fruit and fish are used a lot in Italian cooking. These foods, as well as salamis and other meats, are often bought in open-air or covered markets. There are not as many supermarkets and hypermarkets in Italy as there are in some other European countries. This is especially true of the southern areas.

There are regular 'flea markets' in many of the larger cities. These are markets where people come to buy and sell almost anything.

*The Via dei Condotti shopping street in Rome.*
- *Gucci [GOO-chy] is a well-known shop which sells expensive clothes and jewellery.*
- *There are Gucci shops in other Italian cities and in other countries.*

# ITALIAN COOKING

## Cooking pasta

Italian restaurants have brought Italian cooking to people all over the world. Dishes such as *spaghetti alla bolognese*, *lasagne* and *pizza* are eaten almost everywhere. Italian *minestrone* soup can be bought in packets wherever there are supermarkets. Italian wines are popular around the world.

Many Italian dishes are a rich mixture of meats, cheeses, vegetables and different types of pasta. Pasta is made from flour ground from durum wheat and mixed with water. Eggs can be added to make fresh pasta. Other ingredients can be added to make different coloured pasta, such as spinach for green or tomatoes for red.

There are many types of pasta. The word *pasta* simply means paste. *Spaghetti*, a long thin pasta, means 'little string' in Italian. Pasta can also be made to look like shells, thin strips or wide slabs. There are even pieces of pasta that look like butterflies.

*Eating at a restaurant by Lake Como in north-west Italy.*
- *Eating outside is usual in the summer because of the warm weather.*
- *The beautiful scenery of the mountains and lake makes a wonderful dining room!*

**On average, Italians eat an amazing 27 kilos of pasta per person in a year, a world record!**

*Here the mother serves out the pasta to each member of her family.*
- *Pasta is always accompanied by grated parmesan cheese.*

## Meat

There are many Italian recipes that use meat and pasta. *Spaghetti alla bolognese* uses minced meat that is fried in olive oil, mixed with carrots, onions, celery and tomatoes, and served on *spaghetti*. A sprinkling of *parmesan* cheese completes the dish. To make *lasagne*, meat and vegetable sauce is layered with sheets of fresh pasta and cheese. Pasta can also be stuffed with meat or vegetables to make dishes such as *ravioli* and *cannelloni*. *Risotto* is an Italian dish of rice cooked in stock with meat and vegetables.

## Fish

Fish dishes are more popular in the south of Italy where there are many small fishing ports. Sardines, anchovies, tuna and sometimes lobster are caught. In Sicily, a dish called *pesce* [PESH-eh] *spada* is made by grilling swordfish stuffed with *mozzarella* cheese, herbs and brandy. True *mozzarella* cheese is made from buffalo milk.

## After the meal

Ice cream is said to have been invented in Italy in the 18th century. There is a huge range of different flavours and colours of ice cream. Special family recipes for ice cream are often closely guarded secrets.

Meals are often finished with a *cappuccino*. This is made with strong coffee, steamed, frothy milk and a sprinkling of chocolate on top.

*Lunch is often salad with slices of salami or parma ham, with bread and cheese.*
- *Can you see any olives?*

# MADE IN ITALY

## High quality

Italy has a long and successful history of making high-quality goods. During the Middle Ages, towns and cities such as Venice and Florence became famous for making goods such as glass and cloth. These were sold in fairs and markets all over Europe.

Ornamental glass is still made in Venice. Italian cloth and clothes with designer labels, such as Giorgio Armani, are still important **exports**. An annual show in Milan shows off the creations of Italy's top fashion designers to an international audience.

*Making Murano glass ornaments.*
- *Murano is an island in the Venice lagoon.*
- *Glass has been made there since the 13th century.*
- *Hot glass is shaped by blowing down a long tube.*
- *Different pieces are welded together by melting the glass.*

## Raw materials

Industry needs **raw materials** to make goods in factories. It also needs a source of energy to power machinery. Italy does not have much of either. There is some oil and natural gas in the south of Italy but most of Italy's oil has to be **imported.** In the north, fast-flowing mountain rivers are used to make **hydro-electric power**.

Sulphur from volcanic areas is used to make chemicals such as sulphuric acid.

High quality marble from quarries in Carrara has been used in sculptures and buildings for hundreds of years.

**The name FIAT comes from the initials of the Fabbrica Italiana Automobile Torino, which means the makers of Italian cars in Turin. Turin is still the main centre for making FIAT cars.**

Crops and other types of foods are taken to factories where they are **processed**. Tuna and sardines are cooked and canned. Grapes are pressed and processed to make wine. Durum wheat is ground, made into dough and shaped into pasta.

## Cars and computers

Most of the industry in Italy is in the north. The area between Milan, Turin and Genoa makes a triangle of industry.

Motor cars, motorbikes, aircraft and many other types of electronic goods are made in this area. Two of Italy's most well-known companies are FIAT, which make cars, and Olivetti, which make computers. Names such as Ferrari and Lamborghini are known for making the world's most expensive, fastest sports and racing cars. The Italian love of style and looking good is shown in many of the goods they make.

*Making Ferrari cars at Maranello.*
- *The car is the Ferrari Testarossa, one of the world's most expensive cars.*

# TRANSPORT AND TRAVEL

## From Appian Way to *autostrada*

The Romans knew how to build long-distance roads some 2000 years ago. This was the main way that armies could be moved around the vast Roman Empire. The Appian Way was built from Rome to the southern tip of Italy.

Roads were also important for transporting goods for sale. It was said that 'all roads lead to Rome'.

Now, motorists in Italy can drive on one of the best motorway systems in Europe. There are about 6000 kilometres of *autostradas* (motorways). There is a **toll** to pay on most of them. One motorway called the *Autostrada del Sole,* goes the whole length of Italy from Milan to Reggio di Calabria. This is a distance of 1250 kilometres.

There are only a few ways to get into Italy by land across the Alps. One is through the narrow mountain passes, such as the Brenner pass. The other is to travel through one of the tunnels that have been cut through the mountains. The Mount Frejus tunnel was opened in 1980. This takes cars and lorries for almost 13 kilometres under the Alps from France into Italy.

*Streets in Italian cities are often very crowded, so scooters are a popular way for young people to get around.*

## Rail and boat

There is also a railway network for long-distance travel. About 20,000 kilometres of track link all the main towns and cities. About half of the railway lines have been electrified. This makes them faster, cleaner and cheaper to run. A journey from Rome to Palermo on the island of Sicily takes 14 hours by train. This includes a train ferry between the mainland and Sicily. It takes only 60 minutes to fly between the two cities. Other islands, such as Sardinia, are linked to the mainland by ferry boats and hydrofoil boats.

## Traffic chaos

Rome is Italy's centre for business, politics and for culture. There is an underground rail system to help people move quickly around the city. Young people often prefer to travel on scooters. There are so many cars that **pollution** and traffic congestion are serious problems. This is also a concern in many of Italy's historic towns and cities where the streets are very narrow and trap car fumes.

**One of Rome's airports is named Leonardo da Vinci. Few other countries in the world would name an airport after a 15th-century artist and designer!**

*Concrete motorways have changed the appearance of historic cities such as Rome.*
- *Elevated sections of road help give more space for vehicles.*
- *Modern trams run on their own rails through the city.*

# LEISURE AND SPORT

## Watching and playing

When the weather is warm on a summer's evening, Italians like to sit at a table outside a café, often in the central square called the *piazza*. Others go for an evening stroll called the *passeggiata* [passeh-JAta]. A more active thing to do is to play *bocce* [BOcheh] in the park. This is a game of bowls played in a similar way to French *boules*.

Italians also enjoy watching television. For many, the weekly highlight is watching a football match on Sunday afternoon. Popular teams such as Inter-Milan and Naples are among the best in Europe. Many people enjoy gambling on the Italian National Lottery called the *Lotto* and watching it on TV.

Cycle-racing is a popular sport and at weekends there are lots of long-distance races all over Italy. Basketball, baseball and tennis are also popular and many children learn to ski at an early age.

*Venice is one of Italy's most visited cities.*
- *The boats are called gondolas.*
- *An oarsman uses an oar at the stern to propel the boat.*

*Selling leather bags in a tourist area of southern Italy.*
- *Tourists are as happy to browse through the market stalls as the art galleries!*

## Tourism

Tourism brings a lot of money into Italy. Visitors come from all over the world to look at the buildings and art treasures of historic towns such as Venice, Rome, Naples and Florence. The Tower of Pisa is a special tourist attraction. It has been leaning over since it was first built in 1173.

## Holiday time

Italy's long coastline makes it a popular holiday destination. In the west, there are seaside resorts and harbours, such as Portofino, overlooking the Ligurian Sea. Amalfi and the island of Capri are popular tourist spots further south. On the coast of the Adriatic Sea in the east, there are seaside resorts such as Rimini. In fact, so many tourists visit Italian seaside resorts that they have become one of the causes of sea **pollution**, which has become a major problem.

For a different type of holiday, tourists go to the Alpine ski resorts such as Courmayeur in the Val d'Aosta and Livigno in Lombardy. The Italian lakes, such as Como and Maggiore, are picturesque sites set in Alpine valleys, that people have enjoyed coming to for over 150 years.

**In the 1950s and 1960s film-making in Italy rivalled that of Hollywood. So many westerns, set in America, were actually made in Italy that they became known as 'spaghetti westerns'. One of the most famous spaghetti westerns is *A Fistful of Dollars*, which stars Clint Eastwood.**

# CUSTOMS AND ARTS

## Customs and costumes

Punch and Judy puppet shows began in Italy about 400 years ago with a character called *Pulcinella.* At first, the characters were puppets worked by wires. By 1800 in England, the show had become a glove puppet show. *Pulcinella* had become Punch with a wife named Joan or Judy.

All over Italy there are festivals in which people dress up in masks and medieval costumes. There are colourful masked balls in Venice. In Arezzo, there are jousting matches between people dressed up as crusader knights and their enemies, the Saracens. In Florence, a football match is played between teams dressed in medieval costumes. People ride bareback in a horse race around the *piazza* in Siena. The race is called the *palio* and it began in medieval times. Before the race, there is a parade. People wear medieval costumes and wave flags.

*A religious festival in the south of Italy in Calabria.*
- *This festival is led by Roman Catholic priests.*
- *The central idea of the festival is to ask for rain from the Madonna.*

## Opera and artists

Some of the world's best opera composers and singers have come from Italy. Italian painters and sculptors have created some of the world's greatest masterpieces. The ceiling of the Sistine Chapel in the Vatican City was painted by Michelangelo. It took him four years to complete, between 1508 and 1512. He had to paint while lying on his back up a 20-metre scaffold. Leonardo da Vinci was another great artist, inventor and scientist of the time. The *Mona Lisa* is one of his best-known paintings.

### Religion and festivals

Almost all Italians are brought up to be Roman Catholics and many Italian festivals are connected with the Roman Catholic religion. There are local saints' days and other religious events throughout the year. A music festival is held during Easter week in Assisi, the home of St Francis. Some festivals combine Roman festivals with later Christian festivals. The festival of *Ferragosto* in August recalls the Roman Emperor Augustus, as well as the Virgin Mary.

Each town in Italy has its own saint. Many towns celebrate their saint's day with a festival, when a statue of their saint is carried through the streets.

*The ceiling of the Sistine Chapel painted by Michelangelo.*
- *The Sistine Chapel is part of the Vatican Palace in the Vatican City.*

Different types of food are linked to these religious festivals. For example, marzipan or chocolate lambs are made to eat after Lent, a time when Catholics give up luxuries such as chocolate.

On New Year's Day, the Pope gives a blessing to people all over the world from a balcony in the Vatican City. People crowd into St Peter's Square to hear him give this blessing.

**During Lent, the 40 days before Easter, many Christians fast. This means that they stop eating meat, or luxuries like chocolate. The last days of Lent became known as *Carne vale*, which means 'goodbye to meat', and this is where the word 'carnival' came from.**

29

# ITALY FACTFILE

**Area** 301,270 square kilometres
**Highest point** Monte Rosa 4634 m

## Climate

|  | January temp. | July temp. | Total annual rainfall |
|---|---|---|---|
| Milan | 2°C | 25°C | 1017 mm |
| Rome | 7°C | 25°C | 657 mm |
| Palermo | 10°C | 25°C | 709 mm |

**Population** 57 million
**Population density** 194 people per square kilometre

## Life expectancy
Female 80
Male 73

**Capital city** Rome

## Population of the main cities (in millions)
| | |
|---|---|
| Rome | 2.7 |
| Milan | 1.4 |
| Naples | 1.2 |
| Turin | 1.0 |
| Palermo | 0.7 |
| Bari | 0.4 |
| Bologna | 0.4 |
| Catania | 0.4 |
| Florence | 0.4 |
| Venice | 0.3 |

## Land use
| | |
|---|---|
| Farming | 57% |
| Forest | 23% |
| Other | 20% |

## Employment
| | |
|---|---|
| Services | 59% |
| Industry | 32% |
| Farming | 9% |

## Main imports
Machinery and transport equipment
Manufactured goods
Chemicals
Oil and other mineral fuels
Iron and steel

## Main exports
Machinery and transport equipment
Manufactured goods (electrical goods, clothes and shoes)
Chemicals
Food and drinks

## Language
| | |
|---|---|
| Italian | 94% |
| Sardinian | 3% |
| Other | 3% |

## Religions
| | |
|---|---|
| Roman Catholic | 83% |
| Non-religious and others | 17% |

## Money
The lira

**Wealth** $19,620
(The total value of what is produced by the country in one year, divided by its population and converted into US dollars).

# GLOSSARY

**active volcano** a volcano that is still likely to erupt

**average temperature** the typical amount of heat between the hottest and coldest times of the month

**capital city** the city where a country has its government

**citrus fruits** fruits such as oranges, lemons and limes that contain citric acid

**city states** small countries with a city at their centre

**commercial** different types of business

**dictator** a ruler with complete power over a country

**drought** a long period without rain

**earthquake** violent shaking of the ground

**exports** goods sent out of a country to be sold to other countries

**fasting** avoiding all or some kinds of food and drink, often for religious reasons

**freezing point** 0°C, the point at which water becomes frozen

*garrigue* scrub and grass in a very dry area

**gully** a narrow trench cut into the ground by fast-flowing water

**hydro-electric power** electricity made by harnessing water power

**imports** goods brought into a country to be sold there

**irrigation** watering system set up to water the land

**lava** molten rock that flows out of a volcano

*maquis* trees, scrub and grass in a dry area

**Mediterranean climate** a type of climate experienced in countries around the Mediterranean Sea and on the western side of continents on the same latitude

**peninsular** a long area of land that is surrounded on three sides by the sea

**pollution** different ways in which water and air are made dirty

**processed** making a product from a raw material

**raw materials** the materials needed to make things

**relief** the slopes and shape of the land

**Renaissance** a time in European history during the 15th and 16th centuries

**republic** a country without a king or queen ruling it

**reservoir** a large natural or man-made lake used as a water supply

**Roman Empire** the area once ruled by the Romans

**soil erosion** wearing the soil away

**standard of living** the measure of how well people live and eat in a country

**states** independent countries

**tenements** large buildings divided into flats

**toll** a charge to travel on a road

**tributaries** small rivers that join larger rivers

**vendors** people who sell things

# INDEX